First Pets
Presidential Best Friends

Written by Nell Fuqua
Illustrated by Zina Saunders
Designed by Michelle Martin

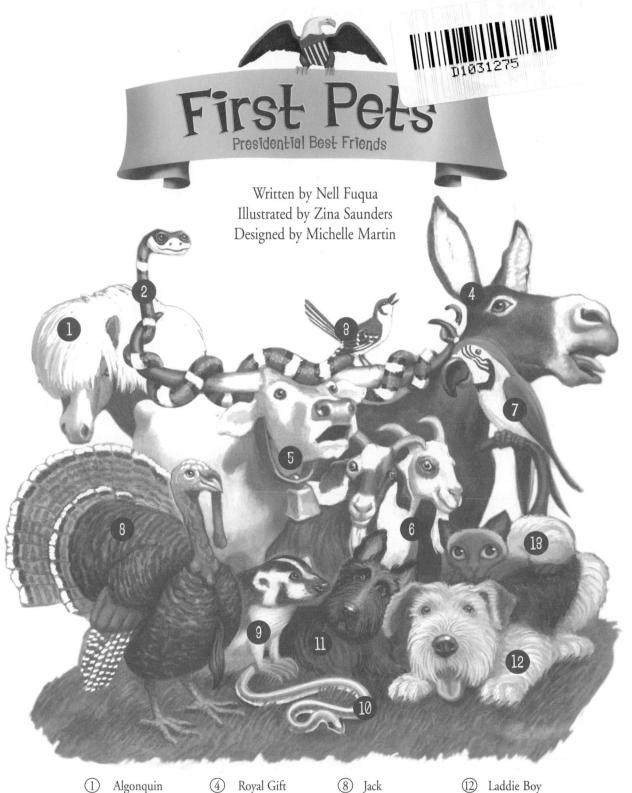

①	Algonquin	④	Royal Gift	⑧	Jack	⑫	Laddie Boy
②	King snake	⑤	Ofelia	⑨	Josiah	⑬	Siam
③	Dick	⑥	Nanny & Nanko	⑩	Emily Spinach		
		⑦	Eli Yale	⑪	Fala		

Copyright © 2004 Scholastic Inc.
Published by Lemon Drop Press, an imprint of Scholastic Inc.
557 Broadway, New York, NY 10012

ISBN 0-439-59846-X

1 3 5 7 9 10 8 6 4 2

Since the founding of our country, pets have played an important role in the lives of our first families. They offer sympathy and unconditional love during stressful times, as well as friendship and entertainment during good times. More than 400 animals have been the best friends of our presidential families. From mice to bears, and from lizards to goats, the variety of these animals is amazing.

Which **bird** tweaked the president's ear, but sang beautifully for the first lady?

Which **pony** sneaked into the White House elevator to cheer up a sick child?

Which **African animal** was the most popular resident of the Washington Zoo for nearly 40 years?

Paw through the book to find out!

1st

George Washington

Term in office:
1789—1797

His Pets:

Birds	1
Dogs	36
Donkeys	4
Horses	Many
Mules	Many

Nelson was George Washington's favorite horse. The chestnut hunter was as brave as his master! He remained calm and obedient during the gunfire and confusion of the worst battles. In recognition of his service, Nelson was retired to pasture at Mount Vernon after the Revolutionary War. He was never ridden or required to work again.

With names such as **Sweetlips** and **Madame Moose**, it's easy to see that dogs held a special place in Washington's heart. Over time, Washington crossed stag hounds with Virginia hounds to create the first foxhound—still used in foxhunts today.

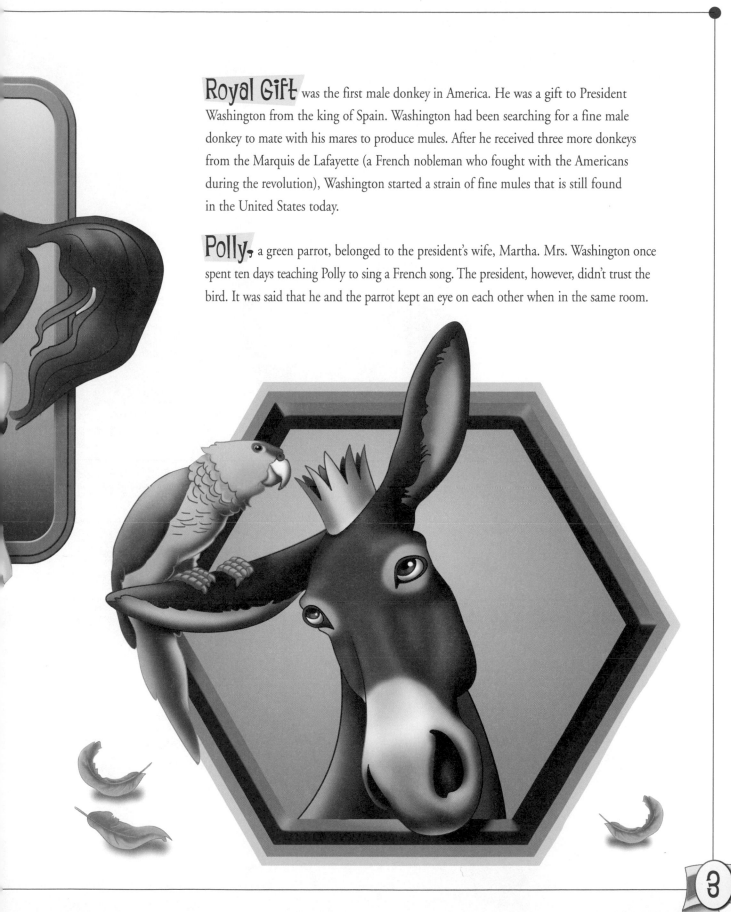

Royal Gift was the first male donkey in America. He was a gift to President Washington from the king of Spain. Washington had been searching for a fine male donkey to mate with his mares to produce mules. After he received three more donkeys from the Marquis de Lafayette (a French nobleman who fought with the Americans during the revolution), Washington started a strain of fine mules that is still found in the United States today.

Polly, a green parrot, belonged to the president's wife, Martha. Mrs. Washington once spent ten days teaching Polly to sing a French song. The president, however, didn't trust the bird. It was said that he and the parrot kept an eye on each other when in the same room.

3rd

Thomas Jefferson

Term in office:
1801—1809

His Pets:

Birds 3

Dogs 2

Bears 2

Horses 9

Dick was a mockingbird, and Thomas Jefferson's favorite pet. He rode on the president's shoulder and learned to take food from Jefferson's lips! One of Dick's favorite tricks was to sing along with the president when he played his violin. When the president went upstairs to bed, Dick hopped up after him, one step at a time.

Imagine having **Grizzly Bears** on your lawn! President Jefferson did, at least for a while.
He had received the two animals as cubs in 1807 from a Western explorer named Zebulon Pike.
He housed them in a cage on the lawn, where the display became known as "Jefferson's bear garden."
The bears showed Americans that new and exciting worlds awaited discovery west of the Mississippi River.
When winter arrived, Jefferson sent the grizzlies to a friend in Philadelphia for full-time care.

Dolley Madison's parrot lived an exciting life. **Polly** was a green macaw, a very uncommon bird in early America. But during the War of 1812, the excitement got out of hand. British soldiers were marching toward Washington, D.C., and President Madison left to check on troops that were defending the capital. Suddenly, the British were very close! Dolley packed up her carriage with items she couldn't bear to leave behind. She took the Declaration of Independence, the household silver, red velvet drapes, a small clock, a portrait of George Washington, and Polly. Just a few hours later, the British arrived and ransacked the presidential home before setting it on fire. Polly had barely escaped with all her feathers!

4th

James Madison

Term in office:
1809—1817

His Pets:

Birds   3

Declaration of Independence

John Quincy Adams

Term in office:
1825—1829

His Pets:

Dogs   1

Odd Pets   Alligator

Of all the pets that have lived in the White House, one of the strangest was an **alligator.** He was caught in Florida while still a baby, and was presented to the Marquis de Lafayette as a gift. Lafayette didn't think it would be polite to turn down a gift, so he took the alligator with him all the way back to Washington! President Adams let the alligator stay in the bathtub in the East Room for months before Lafayette left to return to France. Adams most likely donated the reptile to a zoo.

7th

Andrew Jackson

Term in office:
1829—1837

His Pets:

Birds   1

Horses   5

Odd Pets   Gamecocks

1ST

Truxton was one of the most famous racehorses of his time, but he started off as a loser! The beautiful bay stallion got his lucky break in 1805 when Andrew Jackson saw him lose a race in Nashville, Tennessee. The stallion came in second to the local favorite, Greyhound, but Jackson didn't care. He knew right away that Truxton was special. He bought the five-year-old horse and started him on a tough training routine. Jackson scheduled a re-match with Greyhound, and Truxton came through with flying colors. After Truxton retired from racing, he sired more than 400 foals!

Poll the parrot had a colorful personality. Before he was president, Andrew Jackson took Poll to his home, The Hermitage. After his presidency ended, Jackson returned to Poll and The Hermitage. Poll was even present at his old friend's funeral, for awhile anyway. According to one eyewitness, the bird had to be removed when he let loose with a string of very loud curse words.

10th

John Tyler

Term in office:
1841—1845

His Pets:

Birds 2

Dogs 2

Horses 1

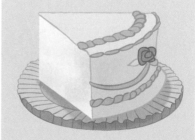

Johnny Ty, a canary, was the victim of a mail-order matching service gone wrong. He belonged to John and Julia Tyler, who had recently married in the White House. The Tylers thought Johnny Ty should have a mate too, so the first lady wrote to her family in New York and asked them to find Johnny Ty a wife. Her family found a beautiful bird and shipped it to the Tyler home in Virginia. Johnny Ty was excited to see another bird being brought into his cage! But something was terribly wrong. Suddenly Johnny jumped off his perch, sat on the bottom of the cage, and hid his head under his wing. Within a week, Johnny was dead. Upon inspection, his owners found that they had given him another male as a mate.

Zachary Taylor

Term in office:
1849—1850

His Pets:

Horses 1

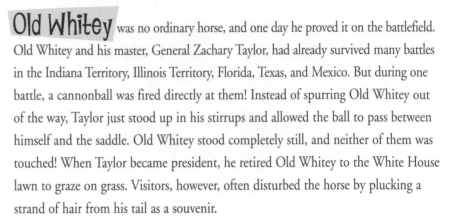

Old Whitey was no ordinary horse, and one day he proved it on the battlefield. Old Whitey and his master, General Zachary Taylor, had already survived many battles in the Indiana Territory, Illinois Territory, Florida, Texas, and Mexico. But during one battle, a cannonball was fired directly at them! Instead of spurring Old Whitey out of the way, Taylor just stood up in his stirrups and allowed the ball to pass between himself and the saddle. Old Whitey stood completely still, and neither of them was touched! When Taylor became president, he retired Old Whitey to the White House lawn to graze on grass. Visitors, however, often disturbed the horse by plucking a strand of hair from his tail as a souvenir.

15th

James
Buchanan

Term in office:
1857—1861

His Pets:

Birds   2

Dogs   1

Odd Pets   Eagles

Lara, a Newfoundland, was probably the largest dog ever to live in the White House. He weighed about 170 pounds (77 kg) and had a huge tail. Lara became a White House celebrity, famous for his strange habit of lying still for hours, with one eye open and one eye closed. "Newfies" were bred as seagoing dogs. They hauled fishing nets out to sea and back to the boat. They are so large and furry that they have been mistaken for bears!

16th

Abraham Lincoln

Term in office:
1861—1865

His Pets:

Birds | 1

Cats | 1

Dogs | 2

Goats | 2

Horses | 3

Ponies | 2

Rabbits | 2

Fido, a mongrel yellow dog, was left behind in Springfield, Illinois, when the Lincoln family moved to Washington, D.C. Lincoln was afraid that Fido would not survive the long train trip, so he entrusted his favorite pet to the Rolls, a neighbor family. This family was asked never to scold Fido for entering the house with muddy paws, and never to tie him up alone in the backyard. Fido was to be allowed into their home whenever he scratched at the front door, and into the dining room at mealtimes. To make the dog feel at home, the Lincolns gave the Rolls their horsehair sofa!

President Lincoln's son Tad had two goats named **Nanny & Nanko,** which were given the freedom of the White House. They were even allowed to sleep on his bed! Tad liked to hitch them to a chair and race his homemade chariot through the halls. Once he hitched them up and drove them through a room where First Lady Mary Lincoln was giving a tea party. President Lincoln said they were "the kindest and best goats in the world."

But wait, there's more...

13

A turkey was presented to the White House as Christmas dinner, but Tad Lincoln grew attached to him and named him **Jack.** When he saw that preparations were being made to kill the turkey, he interrupted a cabinet meeting and asked the president to spare the turkey's life. Lincoln wrote a stay of execution, and Jack became part of the family. It has become a tradition for the president to pardon a turkey each year at Thanksgiving—and it all began with Jack and President Lincoln.

Andrew Johnson

Term in office:
1865—1869

His Pets:

Odd Pets   Mice

Pet **mice?** And wild ones at that? Strangely enough, it's true. Andrew Johnson was enduring lengthy hearings over the job he was doing as president, and the stress was getting to him. One summer night, he showed his secretary a bushel of wheat flour from one of his mills in Greeneville, Tennessee. Johnson explained that the night before he had found a few mice scurrying about, and had left a handful of flour for them to eat. Now he intended to leave a basket for them, as well as a bowl of water on the hearth. The next day, his secretary asked Johnson about his little friends. "The little fellows gave me their confidence," answered the president. Even though we don't know if he named the mice, we can be sure that he found comfort in their company during a very difficult time.

18th

Ulysses S. Grant

Term in office:
1869—1877

His Pets:

Birds   1

Dogs   Several

Horses   10

Ponies   3

Odd Pets   Gamecocks

Cincinnati was a black thoroughbred so adored by his master that almost no one else ever got to ride him. Ulysses S. Grant got the horse when he was still a general. It was presented to him by an admirer, a Missouri man named S.S. Grant, who made the general promise that the horse would never be treated badly. The general readily agreed. After all, Cincinnati was the son of Lexington—the fastest four-mile thoroughbred in the United States! Abraham Lincoln, who was president at the time Grant received the horse, got to ride Cincinnati nearly every day. But Grant rarely let anyone else mount the horse. Over time, Grant became known as the best horseman of all the presidents. He shared the credit with Cincinnati, saying that Cincinnati was the finest horse he had ever seen. During his second term in office, Grant had a statue made of himself on Cincinnati.

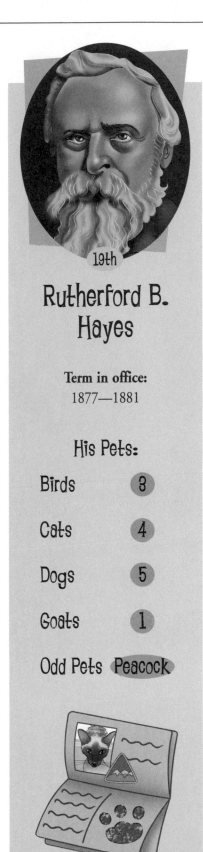

19th

Rutherford B. Hayes

Term in office:
1877—1881

His Pets:

Birds   3

Cats   4

Dogs   5

Goats   1

Odd Pets   Peacock

Siam was the first Siamese kitten ever brought to the United States, and what a journey she had! She was a gift to First Lady Lucy Hayes from David Sickels, the U.S. consul in Siam (now called Thailand). Siam had to be shipped first to Hong Kong, then all the way to San Francisco, and finally across the country to Washington, D.C. Siamese cats were bred by royal families in Siam, and were even known to kill cobras in the gardens of their royal owners!

17

20th

James
Garfield

Term in office:
1881—1881

His Pets:

Dogs   1

Fish   Several

Horses   3

Kit was a handsome brown mare owned by Molly Garfield, President James Garfield's daughter. Molly rode sidesaddle, like most girls of her day. One day a stable hand didn't tighten the saddle properly, and while Molly was riding the saddle slipped and tilted. Kit got spooked and began to run wildly. Molly was thrown from the saddle, but her foot got caught in the stirrup. After a few minutes someone caught Kit's bridle and the screaming Molly was saved. Molly wasn't hurt, but she was so scared that she never rode again.

Grover Cleveland

Term in office:
1885—1889;
1893—1897

His Pets:

Birds   5

Dogs   2

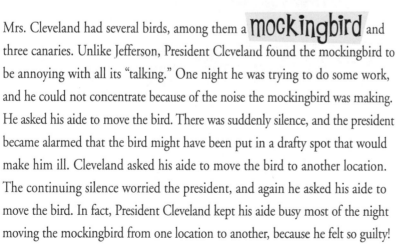

Mrs. Cleveland had several birds, among them a **mockingbird** and three canaries. Unlike Jefferson, President Cleveland found the mockingbird to be annoying with all its "talking." One night he was trying to do some work, and he could not concentrate because of the noise the mockingbird was making. He asked his aide to move the bird. There was suddenly silence, and the president became alarmed that the bird might have been put in a drafty spot that would make him ill. Cleveland asked his aide to move the bird to another location. The continuing silence worried the president, and again he asked his aide to move the bird. In fact, President Cleveland kept his aide busy most of the night moving the mockingbird from one location to another, because he felt so guilty!

squawk!
squawk!

23rd

Benjamin Harrison

Term in office:
1889—1893

His Pets:

Dogs **1**

Goats **1**

Horses **4**

Odd Pets **Opossums**

Of all the goats that have lived at the White House, one stands out as the champion rascal: **His Whiskers.** President Benjamin Harrison liked to give his grandchildren presents and pets, and His Whiskers was one of their favorites. The billy goat would often pull the grandchildren around the White House in a little cart. One day, the stable hands harnessed His Whiskers to the cart and the grandchildren climbed on. But suddenly His Whiskers saw an open gate and made a dash for freedom, with Harrison's grandchildren still in the cart behind him. Harrison ran to catch them, waving his cane and clutching his top hat. The goat didn't stop for several blocks—long enough for many people to see the president chasing a runaway goat down Pennsylvania Avenue.

PENNSYLVANIA AVE.

William McKinley

Term in office:
1897—1901

His Pets:

Birds   1

Cats   5

Washington Post was a clever and magnificent parrot. He was described as a "Mexican double-yellow-headed parrot" by a newspaper, and was worth several thousand dollars. President McKinley was so proud of the bird that he placed the cage where visitors could pass by. Washington Post sure knew how to please an audience. He could finish any song the president began, but he had one special trick. Every time a group of women passed by his cage, no matter how old they were, the parrot would cock his head to one side and cry, "Oh, look at all the pretty girls!"

Oh, look at all the pretty girls!

26th

Theodore Roosevelt

Term in office:
1901—1909

His Pets:

Bears	5
Birds	3
Cats	2
Dogs	5
Horses	10
Pigs	1
Ponies	1
Rabbits	1
Snakes	1

Odd Pets

Badger, barn owl, bobcat, coyote, eagle, flying squirrel, guinea pigs, horned toad, hyena, kangaroo rat, piebald rat, zebra

Algonquin was an Icelandic pony, and the favorite pet of Roosevelt's son Archie. One time Archie got a case of measles, and his younger brother Quentin decided nothing would make Archie feel better than a visit from Algonquin. With the help of a groom, Quentin and his brothers sneaked Algonquin onto the White House elevator to take him to Archie's room. But Algonquin was so enchanted by the mirror in the elevator that they almost couldn't get him out!

Eli Yale was a stunning blue macaw, and belonged to Ted Roosevelt, Jr., the president's son. His beak was large and very sharp, and President Roosevelt said he thought Eli could bite through steel. Even though Eli was very gentle and tame with Ted, the president didn't trust that strong beak, and viewed the bird "with dark suspicion."

Josiah was just a baby badger when a girl in Kansas gave him to President Roosevelt. Josiah (also called "Josh") liked to be held and snuggled. He squealed when he was hungry, and was fed potatoes and milk from a bottle until his teeth grew in. Roosevelt said Josiah looked like a flat mattress with a leg under each corner. When let out of his cage, the badger liked nothing better than to nip at the legs of everyone present. That didn't stop the children at the White House from enjoying him. They simply took Roosevelt's advice to "skip lively!" to avoid Josiah's sharp teeth.

But wait, there's more...

Emily Spinach was a small, green garter snake owned by Roosevelt's daughter, Alice. The snake got her name because Alice said she was "green as spinach and thin as my Aunt Emily." It was very unusual for a girl to own a snake and rumors began to spread. Some people even thought Alice also owned a constrictor!

Snakes were popular with other Roosevelt children, too. One time a local pet store owner allowed Roosevelt's son Quentin to take a **king snake** and two small snakes home for the day. When Quentin burst into his father's study to show them off, the king snake started trying to eat the smaller snakes! It got even worse when the 4-foot king snake went up Quentin's sleeve. A congressman quickly had to overcome his own fear of snakes to help Quentin take off his jacket and get the reptile out.

27th

William Taft

Term in office:
1909—1913

His Pets:

Cows   2

Dogs   2

Pauline Wayne was the last dairy cow to live with a presidential family. Pauline, a handsome Holstein, used to graze on grass near the White House. At night, she retired to her home in a garage, which used to be the stables. There she kept company with President Taft's cars: a White Streamer, two Pierce Arrows, and a Baker Electric. One day the garage was torn down, and Pauline moved—with the cars—to a new building. But she always came "home" to graze on her favorite green grass.

28th

Woodrow Wilson

Term in office:
1913—1921

His Pets:

Birds   2

Cats   1

Sheep   14

Old Ike was a scruffy old ram who liked to chew tobacco. He headed up a flock of sheep on the White House lawn. President Wilson purchased Ike and 13 ewes to replace the gardeners, because of a manpower shortage during World War I. The idea was for the sheep to keep the grass trimmed, but the sheep went too far! Not only did they eat the grass, but they also ate expensive shrubbery and flowers. However, the sheep gave more to the war effort than lawn trimming. Every now and then, the sheep were sheared and their wool auctioned off. Profits went to the Red Cross. One report says that during their stay at the White House, the sheep helped earn $100,000 for the Red Cross.

Warren Harding

Term in office:
1921—1923

His Pets:

Birds	2
Dogs	2

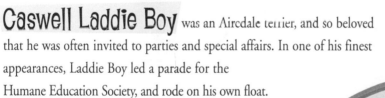

Caswell Laddie Boy was an Airedale terrier, and so beloved that he was often invited to parties and special affairs. In one of his finest appearances, Laddie Boy led a parade for the Humane Education Society, and rode on his own float.

Laddie Boy sat in on cabinet meetings, and had his own hand-carved chair. One time, the Washington Star printed a mock interview with Laddie Boy, who gave his "opinion" about President Wilson's sheep, Prohibition, dog biscuits, a ban on Mexican hairless dogs, and the work hours for guard dogs. When the president died unexpectedly, the Newsboys Association asked every newsboy in the country to donate one penny. The pennies were melted down and made into a statue of Laddie Boy, which can still be seen at the Smithsonian Institution.

30th

Calvin Coolidge

Term in office:
1923—1929

His Pets:

Bears   1
Birds   7
Cats   3
Dogs   12
Donkeys   1
Raccoons   2

Odd Pets

Antelope, bobcat, lion cubs, mynah bird, pygmy hippo, troupial, wallaby

President Coolidge bought two beautiful dogs from a breeder after seeing white collies perform at Ringling Brothers Circus. **Prudence Prim** was the favorite of the president's wife, Grace Anna Goodhue Coolidge. The first lady made large floppy hats trimmed in ribbons for Prudence, who wore them to garden parties at the White House. **Rob Roy** was President Coolidge's favorite. Mrs. Coolidge had her portrait painted with the handsome white collie. It can still be seen in the White House.

Rebecca the raccoon started off as a menu item for Thanksgiving dinner! But President Coolidge had a better idea. He had a special little house built for Rebecca, and walked her around the White House on a leash. Rebecca entertained him by playing happily in a tub of water, swishing around a bar of soap to make bubbles. When the White House was being remodeled and the first family had to move out for awhile, the president worried that Rebecca might not have enough food to eat or enough soap to play with. He sent a limousine to pick up Rebecca so she wouldn't be lonely.

But wait, there's more...

President Coolidge had many odd pets. Most of them were gifts, and after he thanked each animal's owner, he sent the animals to a zoo.

Do-Funny was a trained troupial (a tropical bird similar to an oriole) from South America. Do-Funny would sit on the president's shoulder and tweak his ear, but showed his love for Mrs. Coolidge by calling to her in a flute-like voice.

Coolidge received a pair of lion cubs from the mayor of Johannesburg, South Africa, and named them **Tax Reduction** and **Budget Bureau.**

Smoky, a bobcat, was a gift from the Great Smoky Mountains Association. He was the largest bobcat ever captured in his home county in Tennessee. Smoky was later donated to the zoo, along with the other strange pets.

A pygmy hippo, named **Billy,** was about the size of a dog. He was the most popular animal at the Washington Zoo for almost 40 years. Nearly all the pygmy hippos in zoos across America are descended from Billy.

31st

Herbert Hoover

Term in office:
1929—1933

His Pets:

Dogs   9

Odd Pets   Opossum

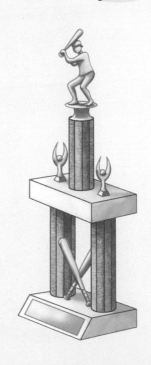

An **opossum** may seem like a dull pet, but the one that President Herbert Hoover "adopted" one day created quite a stir—and not just for the president. The opossum became Hoover's pet after it was found wandering the White House grounds. Unfortunately, it looked just like Billy, an opossum that had disappeared from Hyattsville, Maryland. Billy was the mascot of a baseball team there, and when the team's boys saw Hoover and his pet in the newspaper they believed the opossum was their Billy. The team sent some boys to the White House to identify the opossum, but the crafty animal hid. The boys left a note asking Hoover to send them the opossum for good luck. The president did, and the team reached the state championships.

32nd

Franklin Delano Roosevelt

Term in office:
1933—1945

His Pets:

Dogs   11

Murray the Outlaw of Fala Hill, President Franklin D. Roosevelt's Scottish terrier, became so famous he starred in a movie and a book. Fala attended an inauguration and accompanied Roosevelt when he signed the Atlantic Charter with British Prime Minister Winston Churchill. Once, Fala even went with the president to the Aleutian Islands, off mainland Alaska. Halfway back from the Aleutians, the president noticed that Fala was missing from the ship! He ordered a battleship to go back and get the dog, costing taxpayers thousands of dollars. Fala slept beside Roosevelt's bed at night, and each morning the president's breakfast tray included a dog biscuit for Fala.

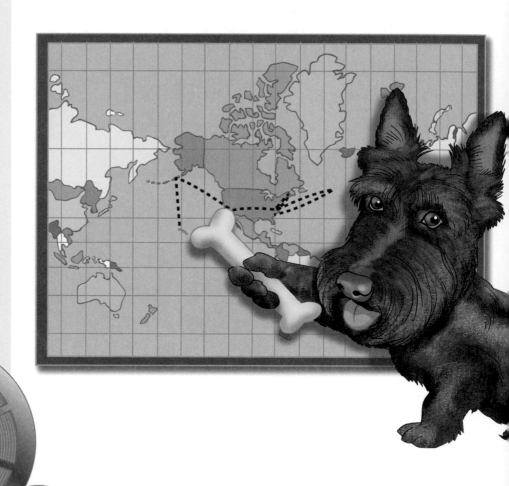

When the United States entered World War II, Fala became an honorary private in the army. After he was photographed giving a dollar to help the war effort, thousands of Fala's fans sent in a dollar, too. Fala also "donated" his rubber chew toys during a scrap drive. Seeing his example, many people donated rubber items as well. The story of his life was written in a book, *The True Story of Fala*.

33rd

Harry S. Truman

Term in office:
1945—1953

His Pets:

Dogs   2

An Irish setter named **Mike** was the only dog allowed during the Truman presidency. President Truman did not like dogs or any other pets. But he finally gave in and let his daughter Margaret accept the puppy from the postmaster general. Mike was not very obedient, and often would not come when called. One night Margaret was chasing him and she noticed a window in the White House with the lights on. She could see maps on the walls and some men in a meeting. She waved and they nervously waved back, then they pulled the shades down. It was a secret map room where they discussed plans for World War II, and she had discovered it by chasing Mike around the White House grounds!

34th

Dwight D. Eisenhower

Term in office:
1953—1961

His Pets:

Dogs   3

Pigs   1

President Eisenhower's favorite dog was a Weimaraner named **Heidi.** In fact, she was the only dog he personally fed. Heidi spent most of her time at the Eisenhower home near Gettysburg, because the fast pace of Washington, D.C., made her nervous. When photographers tried to take a picture of First Lady "Mamie" Doud Eisenhower, Heidi would sometimes jump up in front of her. For some reason, Heidi just couldn't stand to see a camera pointed at the president's wife. Weimaraners were bred in Germany as hunting dogs back in the 1200s. Maybe Heidi preferred chasing rabbits to meeting photographers and reporters.

HEIDI

35th

John F. Kennedy

Term in office:
1961—1963

His Pets:

Birds   3

Cats   1

Dogs   9

Hamsters   2

Horses   1

Ponies   3

Odd Pets   Irish deer

Nearly every child wants a pony, and **Macaroni** was the envy of the nation's children. In fact, he received thousands of letters from kids across the country. Macaroni was a gift from Vice President Lyndon Johnson to Caroline Kennedy, the president's daughter. He pulled the Kennedy children around the White House in a sleigh, and it was such a wonderful sight that the first family used a photo of the event on their Christmas card.

Macaroni was allowed to freely roam the White House grounds. One day President Kennedy looked up from his office desk to see Macaroni peeking in his window. The president opened the door and invited the pony inside. But Macaroni just walked away. He missed the chance to be the first pony ever to enter a president's office.

The Kennedy White House had the most unusual dogs of all, including one that some people suspected might be a spy! Caroline received a fluffy white puppy as a gift from Nikita Khrushchev, the leader of the Soviet Union. This puppy was truly unique. She was the daughter of Strelka, the first Russian dog sent into orbit. Named **Pushinka** (Russian for "fluffy"), this puppy was given a complete physical at an army hospital. People worried she might be wearing an instrument to bug secret meetings. When Pushinka finally made it to the White House, **Charlie** (Caroline's Welsh terrier) flipped for her! Soon the couple had four little pups, named Butterfly, White Tips, Blackie, and Streaker. Because they were the grandpuppies of the original space dog, the president called them "pupniks."

36th

Lyndon B. Johnson

Term in office:
1963—1969

His Pets:

Dogs   5

hooowwwlllll

President Johnson liked to show off with beagles **Him** and **Her.** One time when he wanted the dogs to stand on their back legs for a photograph, he pulled up on their long ears. It hurt, and the dogs yelped! Dog lovers from all over the country wrote angry letters to the president.

Yuki was a tiny stray mutt when the president's daughter Luci found him at a gas station. Yuki was white and silky, and the president was often covered with so much white hair that people said he looked like a baking powder biscuit. He taught Yuki to "sing," and when the first lady traveled to Texas, the president and Yuki would howl their song to her over the telephone.

37th

Richard Nixon

Term in office:
1969—1974

His Pets:

Dogs   4

Checkers was a black and white cocker spaniel that saved his master's career. When Richard Nixon was vice president under President Eisenhower, he was caught taking money from secret contributors. He made a famous speech on TV, and said he had received no major donations but had received a puppy. His children loved the puppy and named it Checkers, and he said he would keep it even if people didn't like the idea. The scandal was put to rest, and Ike kept Nixon on the ticket.

38th

Gerald Ford

Term in office:
1974—1977

His Pets:

Cats   1

Dogs   9

Liberty, a golden retriever, was a gift to President Ford from the White House photographer. She became close friends with the president, and was photographed with him swimming, playing, and relaxing in the Oval Office. When Liberty gave birth to eight puppies, she received letters from all over the country. So many people requested a picture of the mother and pups that a special rubber stamp of her paw print was made to stamp each picture with her "autograph."

Jimmy
Carter

Term in office:
1977—1981

His Pets:

Cats   1

Dogs   1

Misty Malarky Ying Yang, a lovely Siamese cat, belonged to Amy Carter, the president's daughter. Misty had the run of the White House until **Grits** arrived. Grits was a mixed-breed puppy given to Amy by her teacher. Unfortunately, Grits liked nothing better than to chase Misty Malarky Ying Yang. He also had a bad habit of soiling the White House rugs. Grits was finally returned to his former owner, and Misty once again ruled supreme.

TO: Amy

40th

Ronald Reagan

Term in office:
1981—1989

His Pets:

Dogs   2

Horses   4

Rex was a Cavalier King Charles spaniel with a taste for the finer things in life. He was a Christmas gift from President Reagan to First Lady Nancy Reagan. The Washington Children's Museum donated a doghouse for Rex. The museum also hired an interior designer named Theo Hayes, who was married to a descendant of President Rutherford B. Hayes. The doghouse was white clapboard with a cedar shingle roof. It had red curtains and framed portraits of President and Mrs. Reagan. President Reagan complained that when he took Rex to Camp David, the dog always ran ahead and beat him to the "shotgun" seat on the helicopter.

George H.W. Bush

Term in office:
1989—1993

His Pets:
Dogs   8

Millie was a playful English springer spaniel who became famous as an author. She was owned by First Lady Barbara Bush and with the help of her mistress, the spaniel "wrote" *Millie's Book*, a dog's-eye view of life in the White House. The book was on the *New York Times* bestseller list for months, and the profits were donated to charity. But before becoming an author, Millie was voted Washington, D.C.'s "ugliest dog." Her picture appeared on the cover of *Washingtonian* magazine, but the magazine later apologized for the insult. It also sent Millie dog biscuits as a peace offering.

Later, Millie had six puppies and her picture was on the cover of *Life* magazine. One of the puppies, Spot, was adopted by the president's son, George W. Bush. After leaving the White House, Millie was photographed with many famous people, including astronauts, kings, queens, and tennis champions.

42nd

Bill Clinton

Term in office:
1993—2001

His Pets:

Cats   1

Dogs   1

Socks, a domestic shorthaired cat, was a stray kitten when Chelsea Clinton, President Clinton's daughter, found him at her piano teacher's house. Socks liked to ride on the president's shoulder around the White House grounds. He also liked to climb on the podium where the president made speeches. A chocolate Labrador puppy soon joined Socks at the White House. The president named him Luke, but changed his name to **Buddy** after receiving hundreds of suggestions for names.

Socks and Buddy received many letters from all over the world. Several of the letters included pictures of pets, and some of them even contained marriage proposals! First Lady Hillary Clinton decided to publish some of the letters that her pets had received. She wrote *Dear Socks, Dear Buddy,* and donated the profits to the National Park Service.

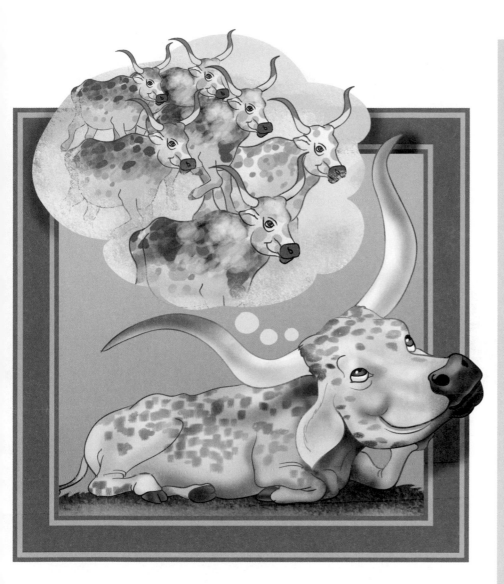

George W. Bush

Term in office:
2001—present

His Pets:

Cats   2

Dogs   2

Odd Pets
Longhorn cow

Crawford

TEXAS·

Ofelia is a black-spotted longhorn cow that lives at President Bush's ranch in Crawford, Texas. The longhorns originally came from Spain and England, and their long legs and hard hoofs were perfect for long cattle drives across the western plains. Many longhorns were rounded up by cowboys and driven to market. But when farmers put up barbed-wire fences, the open range came to an end—and the longhorns nearly became extinct. Ranchers discovered that longhorns are very strong and don't get sick easily. They started raising them again, and now the longhorns are no longer endangered.

But wait, there's more...

Spot "Spotty" Fetcher is the only pet who has lived at the White House under two presidents. Spot was one of Millie's puppies, so it must have seemed familiar when President George W. Bush took her back to the White House for the first time.

India, a black, shorthaired domestic cat, caused a large demonstration in India when the people there learned her name. They thought President Bush was insulting them by naming his cat India. They carried signs that said the Indian people were lions, not cats. But India (the cat) is actually named after former Texas Ranger baseball player, Ruben Sierra, who was called "El Indio."